WHALES

ROBERT STANEK'S WONDERFUL DISCOVERIES SERIES

THE COMPLETE GUIDE FOR BEGINNERS & EARLY LEARNING

Whale. Now there's a magical word. The very thought of a whale, like this humpback whale, is enough to inspire dreams of adventures on the high seas.

Whales come in many sizes, from the relatively small, like this dwarf minke whale at 24 feet (8 meters), to bigger than most people can imagine. How big? Well, consider the blue whale...

The blue whale, shown here, is the biggest, heaviest known animal. Blue whales can grow to 100 feet (30 meters) in length and 440,000 pounds (200 metric tons).

Did you know?

How long is 100 feet? Well, if you've ever played baseball. The distance from home plate to second base typically is 90 feet.

How heavy is 440,000 pounds? Well, that's about 25 African elephants.

Whales, like this gray whale, live in all Earth's oceans and must surface to breathe air. Why? Because, like you, whales are mammals.

Being a mammal also means whales are warm-blooded and feed their young milk. A young whale is called a calf. This is a right whale and her calf.

There are many types of whales, but only two main orders, or groups, of whales. Toothed whales are in the first group. Baleen whales are in the second group. As you can see from this gray whale, baleens are bristle-like hairs in the upper jaw.

Baleen whales, like this humpback whale, break through the water surface with their bodies and use the bristles to filter plankton from the water. Plankton are tiny plants and animals.

Did you know?

The blue whale, the humpback whale, the bowhead whale and the minke whale are baleen whales.

Right whales, Bryde's whales and gray whales also are baleen whales.

Yes, you read that correctly. Enormous whales, like the humpbacks shown here feeding, eat tiny sea animals and plants. Would you ever guess their favorite food is krill? A krill looks like a tiny shrimp.

Although krill are most abundant in the Arctic ocean, not all whales like cold water. This Bryde's whale, which also has baleen, prefers warm tropical and temperate waters. Baleen also is perfect for filtering small fish like sardines.

Baleen whales don't drink the water they filter. When the whale opens its mouth under water, the water pours into its mouth and then the whale pushes the water out through the baleen. This filters the water and what remains is dinner.

Speaking of dinner, toothed whales have a much more varied diet than baleen whales. This sperm whale, which can grow to 42 feet (13 meters), likes to eat giant and colossal squid.

Sperm whales travel in pods and dive to depths of 7,500 feet (2 kilometers) in search of food. They eat large squid, octopus and fish using teeth that weigh up to 2.2 pounds (1 kilogram).

This beluga whale is also a type of toothed whale, as is the narwhal with its long, pointed horn. Like most toothed whales, beluga love to eat fish.

If you think nothing would eat a sperm whale, you haven't met the killer whale. The killer whale, another type of toothed whale, will eat young sperm whales.

Pilot whales also have been known to attack young sperm whales, but mostly they like to eat squid and fish.

Dolphins, killer whales and pilot whales have a large fin on their back. This back, or dorsal, fin helps them swim through the water and makes it easier to make sudden turns.

Dolphins also are a type of toothed whale (but they have their own family tree).

This whale is spouting. Whales spout when they breathe through their blow holes. Baleen whales have two blow holes. Toothed whales have one blow hole.

All whales have front flippers, but humpback whales have the largest flippers. Inside the flippers are bones forming five digits, almost like a hand.

Whales enjoy leaping out of the water. When most of the whale's body comes out of the water, the whale is said to be breaching.

After breaching, whales land on their backs or sides. Often a whale will breach multiple times.

Some whales like to slap their tales hard against the water. This is called slapping or lobtailing. Scientists don't know exactly why whales breach or lobtail.

Some suggest these movements are signals to other whales. Perhaps though, whales are simply trying to say, "Hi, I'm here. Look at me." Or perhaps, they're trying to say, "Goodbye."

Your turn...

In the pages that follow, we'll show you pictures of whales. Do you remember their names?

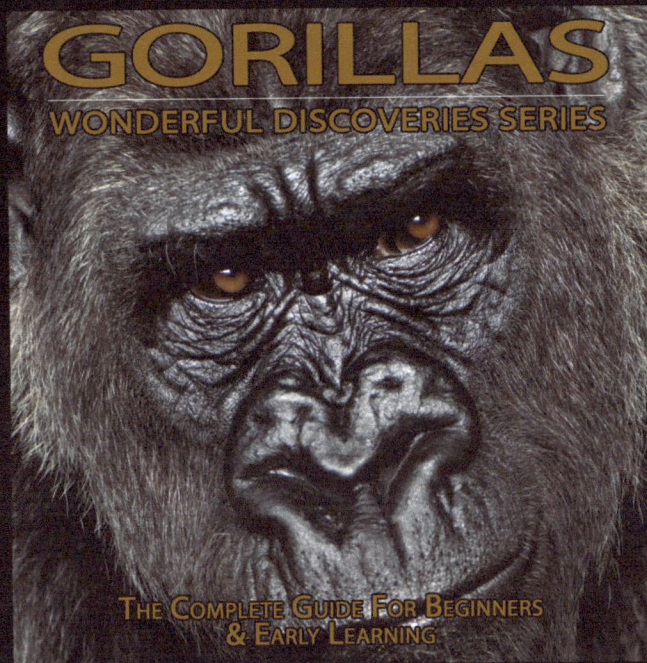

GORILLAS
WONDERFUL DISCOVERIES SERIES
The Complete Guide For Beginners & Early Learning

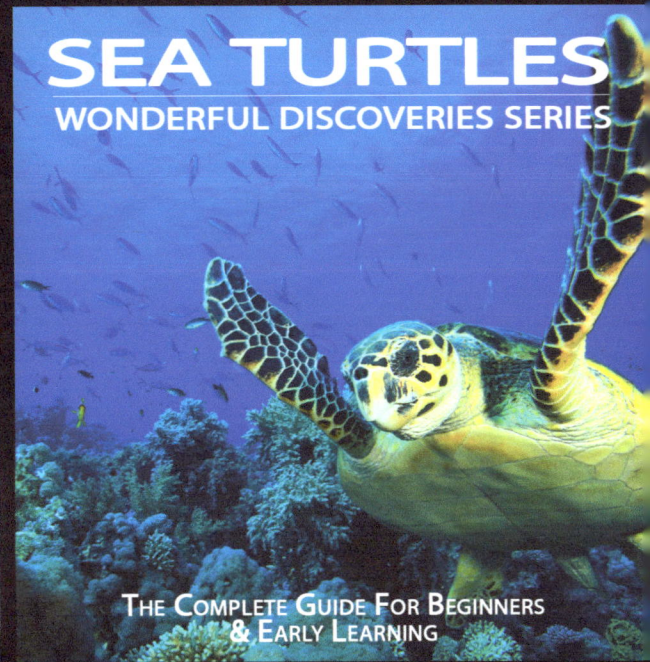

SEA TURTLES
WONDERFUL DISCOVERIES SERIES
The Complete Guide For Beginners & Early Learning

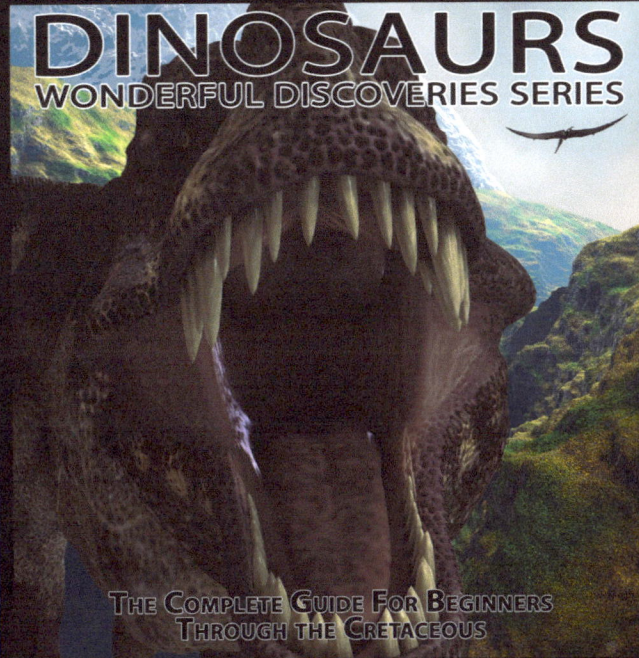

DINOSAURS
WONDERFUL DISCOVERIES SERIES
The Complete Guide For Beginners Through the Cretaceous

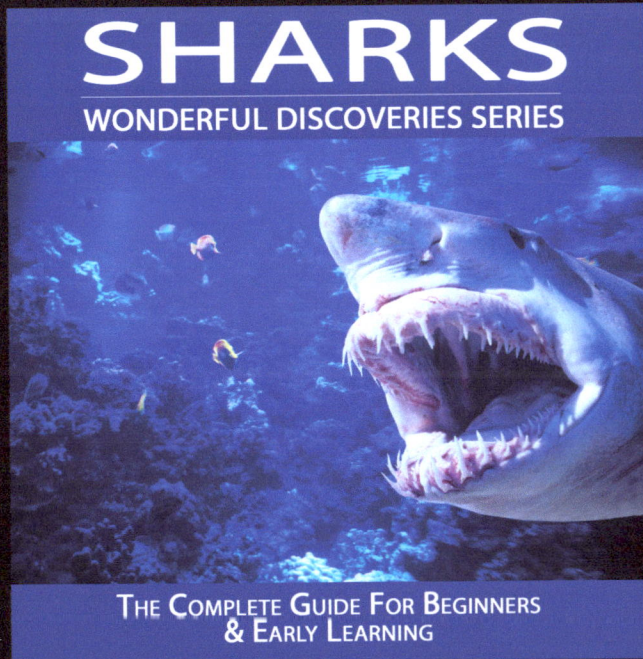

SHARKS
WONDERFUL DISCOVERIES SERIES
The Complete Guide For Beginners & Early Learning

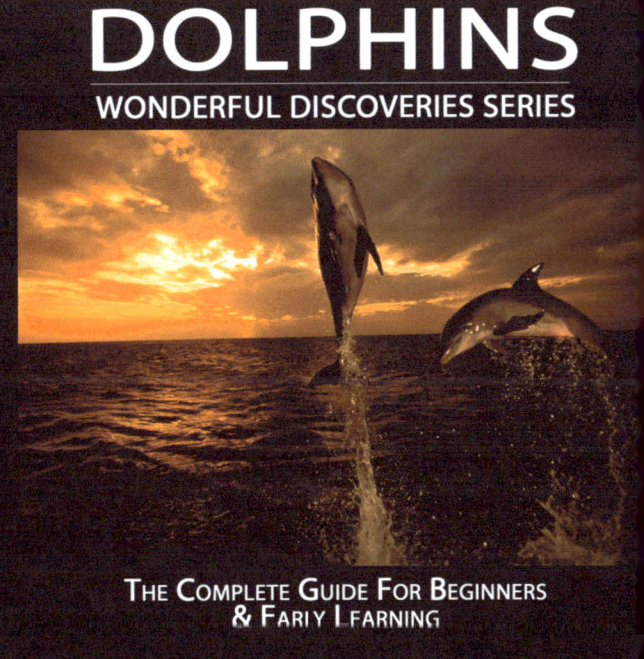

DOLPHINS
WONDERFUL DISCOVERIES SERIES
The Complete Guide For Beginners & Early Learning

WHALES

ROBERT STANEK'S WONDERFUL DISCOVERIES SERIES

Answers:

1. **Killer whales**
2. **Minke whales**
3. **Humpback whales**
4. **Right whales**

THE COMPLETE GUIDE FOR BEGINNERS & EARLY LEARNING

Make sure to check out the other Wonderful Discoveries Series Books!

Originally Published in the United States

First Printing (c) 2021. Robert Stanek's Wonderful Discoveries Series is a trademark of Wonderful World Press. Text copyright (c) 2012 Wonderful World Press. Photographic compilation (c) 2012 Wonderful World Press. Distributed by RP Media.

Page Layout: Creative Design Services
Editorial Production: AP Publishing Solutions

2nd Edition

www.ingramcontent.com/pod-product-compliance
Lightning Source LLC
Chambersburg PA
CBHW040711150426

42811CB00061B/1818

9 781627 165723